MW01206574

The
Invisible
Clock

A practical revolution in finding time
for everyone and everything

George Lawrence-Ell

Kingsland Hall Publishing
a division of Kingsland Hall, Inc.

First published 2001
ISBN: 0-9715396-9-3

This book is dedicated to my sons
Anthony, Michael, and John
who have taught me that time has no limits
and that's where joy is to be found.

"I don't want to be a poet.
I want to change your life."
—Rainer Maria Rilke

Table of Contents

Acknowledgements

This book would not exist without the creative energy, insight, and understanding of my wife Lorraine and my colleagues Bernice Landry and Mark Fenwick.

Many friends on two continents have also contributed their comments, offered encouragement and needed intellectual support, none more so than my sister-in-law Lynne Little and my friend Manfred Schwab.

Honorable mention must go to my mother-in-law Betty and my mother Minna, who never stopped asking when the book was going to be finished. Now I suppose they will want a free copy.

There is a very special meaning to this work because of one person. While I was writing this book, my niece

Lisa Joy passed on to her eternal home. She was only twenty. She left me with a great gift—a renewed sense of mission for my own work as I mourned the loss of watching her life unfold. I want everyone to know that.

Finally, for those who know, thanks to Max, wherever he is, for all the long walks and his very kind attention.

Preface

There is something very disturbing about the way many of us spend and manage our time. We live our lives oscillating between one uncomfortable extreme to the other—rushed and panicked one second, bored and apathetic the next, incapable of adjusting to a speed that suits us. Occasionally we experience moments of clarity and vision, and things run the way we think they should. But these moments don't seem to happen very often or last very long. As a whole we don't know how to act purposefully on a day-to-day, moment-by-moment level.

Our relationship with time is perhaps the most fundamental and problematic of our lives. Time challenges seem to come in almost an infinity of guises. Many of us struggle with experiences in our respective pasts, unable to let go and move on. Some are overwhelmed by many goals and priorities with never enough time in the day to fulfill them all. Others simply feel a nagging sense of detachment, having lost all the immediacy and thrill of living.

All of these different phenomena share one thing in common, the failure to live in the present moment, in the now. Most people realize intellectually that all we have is now. After all, the past is gone forever and the future is uncertain. A seize-the-day mentality, however, is maddeningly difficult to achieve with any degree of consistency. We become easily distracted by memories, dreams for the future, insecurities, and doubts. We veer off course, procrastinate, and wind up doing the same old things we've always done, even if we know they don't add up to truly meaningful lives.

This book is about finding time, so the emphasis shifts from how to become an expert scheduler to understanding our true relationship to time. It is not, however, an abstract intellectual treatise concerning the latest theories in physics. Everything discussed in the following pages deals with, and only with, concrete phenomena observable to everyone. It is a new vision of familiar elements that helps us achieve the goal of living successfully right now.

If you want a book on scheduling this is not the book for you. In many ways this is the antithesis of traditional time-management books because its premise is that your wristwatch is among the last things you should consult when managing your time. For time is not just a number on a clock. It is the series of successive nows through which we live. The moment that you feel right now, and now, and now, is, for all intents and purposes, your time, and consequently, your life. Time is not, therefore, an element outside of yourself, simply the time you see on your watch, but the razor's edge of consciousness that is gone by the time you grasp it.

The central theme of this book is hinged upon one simple, universally observable, yet mostly ignored phenomenon: We experience time as a perception through what we will call an Invisible Clock. Although every day we consult clocks and calendars that keep time in consistent increments of seconds, hours, and days, our actual experience of time, the way we feel about it, is not doled out in measured parts. On the contrary, it fluctuates. One hour in a doctor's office will not feel the same as one hour in the company of a friend. In fact, one hour in a doctor's office will not feel the same as another hour in the same doctor's office. Stop and think about it, and you will no doubt come to the startling conclusion that there is no universal, standard perception of a minute or an hour. No two hours, no two seconds, are perceived exactly the same. They are all unique.

Beginning with an honest look at the limitations of all perceptions, and our perception of time in particular, this book will help guide us to fascinating discoveries about the value, even the necessity, of living in the present moment. For it is precisely the knowledge of our limitations of the perception of time that will free us from our respective pasts, and help us gain the assurance to focus on all we have, which is always right now.

Introduction

∞

"Clock time is our bank manager, tax collector,
police inspector; this inner time is our wife."
— *J.B. Priestley*

Most of us do not think very much about the nature of time. Except for physicists, philosophers, or science fiction writers, the examination of time is considered far removed from the pressing concerns of everyday life. We fail to see how it could benefit us and assume, ironically, that such an endeavor would likely be a waste of time. Yet time considerations are always at the forefront of our minds. Let us stop and examine on how many occasions in an average day we think about time.

Many of us awaken each morning to the aptly named alarm clock, designed to shock us into consciousness, thereby ensuring that our very first consideration of the day is time. We rush to get ready for work, our movements formed into a well-timed routine. We commute, hoping that there will be no accidents or delays so that we will arrive at an agreed-upon time.

At work, we are confronted with a myriad of deadlines that we rush to meet. We wonder how we will find the time to do it all. Or maybe the workflow has slowed a bit, and, in our boredom, we kill some time. Perhaps we wonder if it's the right time to mention that great new idea we had to the manager, or if another time would be better.

We leave our offices at about peak time to fight the traffic, pushing the city's infrastructure to its very limits. At home, we need some "down time" in front of the television before we have some "quality time" with our spouse or kids.

Then, at bedtime, we lie awake wondering if we are advancing in our job at the pace we want. Is it time to ask for a promotion? Time for a change? Finally, we agonize over whether we are spending our precious time in the way we really want, with whom we really want, or if someday we will be filled with regret.

In the last twenty-five years especially, unprecedented scientific developments in communications, travel, and information technology have made the perception of change, and time itself, issues not only for scientists but also for all of us. No one can successfully maneuver in the workforce without becoming adept at time management. It is an essential life skill.

We need look no further than the day planner industry to see how hyper-aware we have become of time. Most of us have forgotten that these gadgets and schedules we carry around were designed to save time. In the vast majority of cases, they seem to have accomplished the opposite. We are more harried and pressed for time than ever. Indeed, we have become time's slaves.

But if the last century has taught us anything, it's that all the gadgets in the world will not lead to the effective management of time. The truth is, time management as it has been traditionally defined—using a watch, calendar, and organizer to manipulate the scheduling of events—will not solve the basic problem of having too much to do and not enough time in which to do it. True time management cannot be achieved merely by juggling schedules. It can only be accomplished by looking frankly at our relationship to time itself.

Instead of being resentful of time pressures, we should view them as an opportunity to re-examine our relationship with time and with ourselves. What creates so much tension between our experience of time and the swiftness of events shaping the world around us? To find the answer, we will have to look at the way we actually perceive time and events. We may be somewhat intimidated by the concept of time, perhaps assuming that such an exploration will lead us to a blackboard full of baffling mathematical equations. But that need not be the case. For we are not attempting to dispute or reinforce Einstein's theories. Instead we will discuss how we actually experience time on a day-to-day practical level, and what is consequently the best way to handle it.

The Invisible Clock is a phrase designed to describe the cognitive mechanism we all have that perceives time. Unlike the clock on the wall, each of us comes equipped with our own Invisible Clock. It ticks away at its own pace depending on what we're thinking or doing. In a way it can be compared to any other sense, like taste or sight. Our Invisible Clock perceives time, just as our ears perceive sound.

Although there is not much we can do to manipulate the essential characteristics of the way we perceive time, we can change how we relate to our Invisible Clock, and consequently how we relate to time itself. We may not like how we perceive time, but if we better understand the dynamics we can form a much healthier relationship with time itself. To this end, we can envision two basic models that will serve to explain how most of us ordinarily relate to time and the better alternative of how we can relate to it now.

The first one, the Time-Driven Mind (*fig. 1,* page 6), illustrates the dynamic that occurs when we are constantly driven by clock time. Our experiences, our perception of the past (chronology), and what's happening now (circumstance), are projected through the narrow passage of measured time. In this model, our thoughts are scattered around multiple priorities, rarely focused on a single one. We are content to become expert multi-taskers and jugglers. Occasionally, often after a crisis, we focus our mind exclusively on one priority. As a rule, though, we oscillate from feelings of apathy to panic. Our ability to succeed in doing the right thing at the right time is hit-and-miss.

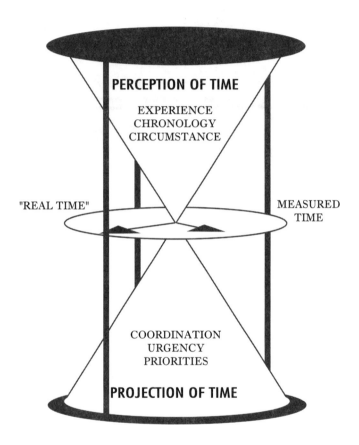

Fig. 1: Invisible Clock model of the Time-Driven Mind

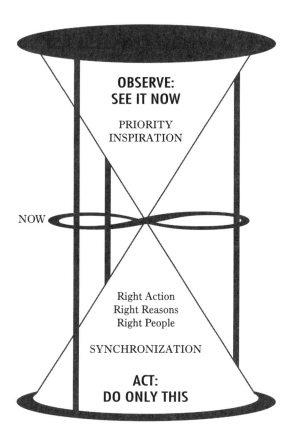

Fig. 2: Invisible Clock model of the Mission-Driven Mind

The Mission-Driven Mind (*fig. 2,* page 7) represents how we function when we are totally focused on the present and consequently become mission-driven. Here our thoughts move through our minds in a fresh way where we don't pre-judge or jump to conclusions. Instead, we separate data that is technically relevant from other psychological interpretations. That familiar feeling of panic is transformed into one of inspiration; we know we are focused on what is right. We are infused with creative energy, and find ourselves taking action and integrating it with the people around us and fully understanding the reasons why.

Do not be concerned if you don't fully grasp the above explanations. The entire book is dedicated to explaining them. Except for the beginning chapters that deal with how we perceive in general, every subsequent chapter will deal with each aspect of both the Time-Driven and Mission-Driven Mind models, and how we will transform from one to the other. It will be advisable to keep track of where you are by referring to these models as you continue to read this book.

Another word on how to get the most out of this book: It is not meant to be a passive experience. Although many of the ideas may not be ones you have considered before, it should not be a theoretical exercise for you. It is designed to help you understand time and ultimately deal with time, your time, on an everyday, practical level. That's why at the end of most chapters you will find questions that will help you to focus on the issues at hand. There are also exercises throughout the book at crucial sections. I urge you not to ignore them but to complete them as best you can.

Chapter 1

∞

THE NATURE OF TIME

"There exists, therefore, for the individual, an I-time, or subjective time. This in itself is not measurable."

—*Albert Einstein*

Time is a phenomenon that at first seems disarmingly straightforward. But the deeper you delve, the more beguiling it becomes. Naturally everyone thinks he understands what time is, and when asked will simply point to the clock on the wall. But the paradoxes of time have both fascinated and frustrated the greatest minds of every civilization since the beginning of recorded time.

It is beyond the scope of this book to discuss the evolution of views on time and how it came to be measured. Nor will we discuss the fascinating labyrinth that leads us to what physicists believe is the correct understanding of time. But we will touch on the discoveries of two titans of scientific genius, Sir Isaac Newton and Albert Einstein.

When it comes to theories of time, these two scientists stand as polar opposites. Newton represents the culmination of a train of Western scientific thought that strove to prove the existence of absolute time. At the end of the seventeenth century it was he who asserted that time is concretely measurable and knowable. He believed that time unravels itself like an arrow through the sky at a fixed rate and in exact, knowable parcels, forever. This in turn led to other assertions that, not only time, but everything is knowable and quantifiable. The mysteries of the universe exist in absolute structure, already immutably formed. All that is left, he argued, is to uncover them.

This idea of absolute time, along with most other Newtonian assumptions, was thought to be true until rival theories were discovered by perhaps the best mind of the last century, Albert Einstein. According to his astonishing

11

theory, the measurement of time is not absolute, but inextricably dependent on motion. The clock literally speeds up or slows down in relation to anything else depending on how fast it is traveling. As a famous example goes, if one person stays fixed on earth, his experience of time would differ relative to his friend who rocketed around the universe at close to the speed of light. The inevitable conclusion is there is no absolute or "right" time—it all depends on individual perspective. In fact, it does not even make sense to refer to time as an independent variable, which is why the phrase "space-time continuum" was born.

Although Einstein's theories are verifiable, they do not have any great bearing on our day-to-day lives since the speed in question has to be immense to even register a slight difference in time. Of course, we don't usually rocket around the universe at close to the speed of light; our collective experience of time remains about the same, and our clocks still work as well as we need them to. Yet these developments in science are invaluable in that they illustrate a paradigm shift in the way time is understood as an absolute, external, objective reality to a relative, internal, subjective reality.

On a personal level, let us examine how much of time we experience as an absolute and how much as relative. Imagine that you look at your day planner and notice that you have two consecutive hour-long appointments. One is an eleven o'clock conference call with a client in another part of the country. The other is a lunch date with a woman who you happen to find fascinating and charming.

Eleven o'clock rolls around and you take a seat in the conference room to wait for the call. Your boss is seated next to you, drumming his fingers on the table. You wish you could be frank and tell him what a huge waste of time you think this meeting will be, but you keep your mouth shut. The person who is supposed to call is late by only a few minutes, but for all of you sitting around aimlessly, it seems like hours. Finally the phone rings, but it's not the person you expected but a guy named Fred, who is the most long-winded, arrogant person imaginable. He irritates you so much that you can't help but tune him out. You stare blankly out the window, wishing you were the window washer you see working on a nearby building. You look back at the clock and realize that only ten excruciating minutes have passed...

Finally, after what seems like infinity and back, the

conference call ends. You dash off to meet your lunch date. She is waiting for you in the lobby wearing a delightful outfit. You are surprised by how excited you are to see her, and, by the look in her eye, she feels the same way. She suggests a deli to go to, and you agree. You sit at the table and are so engrossed in conversation that you fail to notice the waitress standing by, ready to take your order. In what seems like seconds later, the food arrives, and you think to yourself "wow, that was fast!" You listen to what she says, trying to memorize every word so you can go over it later in your mind. Then abruptly she says: "Well, we should be getting back." And you are horrified to realize that your hour with her is almost over.

According to the clock, these two hours passed at the same rate. But the perception of these hours was far from similar. These examples beg the question, if you were asked to describe what an hour feels like, what would you answer? Does it feel the same in a dentist's chair? Watching a movie? On a transatlantic flight? For a kid in the backseat of a car? Over coffee with your best friend? Waiting for your exam marks to be posted?

We all know from practical experience that our sense of time is directly related to what we're doing and thinking. Yet despite the universality of our experience of time as a perception, it can be a difficult idea to accept. We have become accustomed to looking at clock time as the only reality and our individual perception as simply a quirk of the mind. We somehow think that when we glance at the time, we are correcting our "wrong" experience of it.

In fact, we all have an Invisible Clock that reveals our perception of time. Each of our Invisible Clocks determines whether time is passing slowly or quickly for us. While the clock on the wall is an indispensable tool designed to tick away at our best estimation of constant intervals, our Invisible Clock is our own internal reality of how we experience time. No one is arguing that the former is anything but indispensable, but in this book we will also discover the overlooked relevance of the latter.

You may have noticed that when you have a healthy relationship with time, you tend to forget about it. That's because you are doing what you want to do, with little regard for the turning hands of time. In the following pages, you will be able to find the sweet spot where you are ruled by a sense of inspiration rather than the tyranny of clocks and calendars.

Questions

1. How many times a day do you consult your watch?

2. How often do you find yourself pressed for time?

3. How often do you find yourself killing time?

4. When was the last time you were so engrossed in something that you lost track of time?

5. Count the number of calendars, appointment books, day planners, etc. in your home. How many of them do you use?

6. Do you feel guilty if you don't schedule your day?

7. Do you feel disoriented if you don't follow a schedule?

8. How do you feel when your schedule is disrupted?

Chapter 2

∞

THE NATURE OF PERCEPTION

*"If a man will begin with certainties, he shall
end in doubts; but if he will be content to begin
with doubts, he shall end in certainties."*

—Francis Bacon

Before we discuss the role our Invisible Clock plays in our
lives, it is crucial to explain why perceptions are important
and what we mean by perceptions in general. We know
that each of us perceives our surroundings differently, but
what can we say are the common traits of all perceptions?
This topic, which is essential to understanding the true

nature of our Invisible Clock and therefore our ability to successfully manage our time, will be discussed in this chapter and the next.

The human mind and its cognitive abilities are often considered by scientists to be the last mysterious frontier. One reason is the sheer number and range of perceptions we process on a daily basis. It is estimated that a person can have as many as 50,000 thoughts per day, possibly even more. Indeed, the capability of the average mind is truly staggering.

We may not know the exact number of thoughts we have each day, but one thing is certain. All day long we are bombarded with impressions and ideas that we must try to make sense of. And, equally as impressive, our minds seem able to switch gears almost instantly to be able to handle the load. At one moment we might be admiring a particular shade of red, and then, without skipping a beat, we might remember a hurtful comment someone said twenty years ago.

We are so busy with these thoughts that we don't tend to consider why we think them. Nor do we generally attempt to categorize and understand the kinds of thoughts we have. We leave those questions to philosophers or psychiatrists. But we need not be experts on cognition to be aware of what is going on inside our own heads.

We acquire perceptions through our senses—sight, hearing, smell, touch, and taste—and, as a collective, they become the database of information we use to live. The content of the mind is made up of millions of these bits of information and fragments of data. Thinking is the act of processing these perceptions—the way we retrieve information and categorize them in an ever-changing kaleidoscope. Of course, perceptions seem bewildering in their diversity, and scientists certainly have not uncovered all there is to know about them. But they do share some common traits.

Table 1: Characteristics of Perceptions

Incomplete	limited to a single point of view
Variable	by frame of reference
Selective	to confirm pre-existing beliefs

First and foremost, perceptions are limited to a single point of view—our own. Naturally, how we see something will not be the same as how the person standing next to us sees it. Since perception is by definition incomplete in its nature, it is subjective. Or, to put it another way, individual perception constitutes only a limited part of the whole picture.

Secondly, perceptions are variable. They change depending on our point of view and frame of reference. The thing we were looking at yesterday will not, even to us, look exactly the same as it will today. It will vary, sometimes not by very much, sometimes by a lot.

Finally, perceptions are selective. They are influenced by our already existing perceptions. In general, they seek to reaffirm what we already believe. And, as we strive to confirm what we believe, we stack the deck against any conflicting information by either twisting it to fit our interpretation or ignoring it altogether. This offers a sense of security in an ever-changing world. But it does not always help us to see clearly.

Let us explore the variety of ways in which we perceive a single picture.

The Phillips Collection, Washington, D.C.

Exercise 1. Take a sheet of paper and write down what you think is happening in this picture. Look carefully. Study the facial expressions, the smaller details in the picture. When you've finished, turn the picture upside down. What do you see now?

Compare your impressions to these statements made by someone attending one of my seminars: "Someone in that picture, mentioning no names, of course, has had too much to drink. And what's-her-name is as jealous as ever and watching her husband like a hawk. And you would think that the hostess's brother would not be so nosey." Whereas another participant commented: "What a glorious day to be outside—good food, good company, good wine. If only I had been born a century earlier. What a wonderful lifestyle." Their perceptions are so different that it is almost as though they were commenting on two separate paintings.

What information and qualities arise when the picture is right side up, the way we are meant to view it? Here we tend to see the psychological information contained in the story the picture tells us. Of course, since it's a painting, a work of art, we naturally seek out its beauty; and since it's a painting of people, we try and figure out what they're doing. In other words, we look for what is familiar and important to us to confirm our points of view.

But what comes into focus when the picture is turned upside down? Here we tend to see the technical elements—the form, shapes, structure, how these elements fit together, and perhaps even the method the artist used, from the brush strokes to the grand movements created by the geometry and organization of the picture. Why do we tend to focus on these elements instead of the narrative? The reason is that when the normal pattern is disturbed, the story is missing. The messages we are programmed to expect are interrupted.

These are the basic points you should take away from exercise one.

The first is a reminder of something of which all of us should be aware—that there exists an infinity of different points of view. It is a humbling, but verifiable fact that no person possesses the whole picture, each being limited, by definition, to a single and incomplete perspective. No one can ever possess the whole picture.

Secondly, every time you glance at the picture you will notice something else. Look at the same picture more than once and each time you will see it a little differently. Your perception can never remain totally static, but, like all things, it has no choice but to change every moment.

Thirdly, we seek to verify what we already believe. If we have romantic ideas about the past, we will see this picture through primarily those lenses. If we tend to view people as gossipy and jealous, we will assume that these imaginary people are behaving the same way. We all want to confirm what we believe to be true.

Finally, when the way we usually look at the picture is interrupted, we tend to see something different. We see something more. Our mind is compelled to move away from its framework of psychological information to more technically oriented data. We will observe this universal characteristic of our minds again in later chapters.

Not only is it important to become aware of the characteristics of our collective perceptions but we must also observe what we as individuals are perceiving. We will begin along this path by looking directly at our perceptions.

Exercise 2. Write down exactly what you are thinking right now. What have you been thinking in the last ten minutes? Do it as quickly as possible, and take care not censor yourself or what you are thinking in any way.

This is not a test, but simply a demonstration. Ask yourself how many times your mind has wandered since you picked up this book. Did you think about what you're having for dinner? A bill you need to pay? Most of us let thoughts run through our minds without paying them much attention, maybe not even being entirely aware of them. At first you may be surprised by what you notice. It may not be easy to do this, but after you learn how to ambush your own mind, with courage you will be able to do it more easily. As with most things, it's a question of practice.

For the rest of this book, when you come across this symbol, ⧖, take a moment and examine the thoughts traveling through your mind at that instant. This is one of the most important things you can take away from this book—the ability to watch your thoughts without getting lost in them. Remember to abstain from the reflex to judge your perceptions or lie to yourself about them. You cannot predetermine what will pop into your head. The first step to understanding perceptions is to simply observe them without comment.

Questions

1. Have you ever given any thought to the limitations implicit in your own perceptions?

2. Are you stubborn about the validity of your point of view? Or, to put it another way, do you form attachments to your ideas just because they are yours?

3. Do you have an irresistible impulse to argue that you're right?

4. How often have you, in the middle of a disagreement, opted to admit you're wrong and abandon your own point of view?

5. How often each day do you notice your mind wandering?

6. When your mind wanders, does it tend to wander onto the same topics?

7. Do you enjoy new thoughts and experiences, or do they intimidate you?

Chapter 3

∞

CATEGORIES OF PERCEPTION

"Get your facts first, and then you can distort them as much as you please."

—*Mark Twain*

The last chapter discussed the limitations implicit in all perceptions—that they are incomplete, variable, and selective. It also focused on the importance of simply watching your own thoughts without being self-conscious or judgmental. This chapter further expands on the understanding of all perceptions by offering a unique way to categorize them.

Any categorization system which can hope to contain all possible perceptions will be a tricky, even controversial topic. Since it basically concerns almost every human experience, there are many different ways it could be done; in fact, we could easily devote the rest of this book, and many other books besides, to the relative merits of different systems. But that is not our goal. Instead, we will use a working model that will ultimately lead to a better understanding of our Invisible Clock and our ability to get the most out of each moment of time.

We will see that most of our experiences fall into these basic perceptual categories.

Table 2: Categories of Perception

Technical	Psychological	Ego	Time
Reliable	Emotions	Images	Experience
Conditional	Beliefs	Roles	Chronology
	Opinions		Circumstance
	Attitudes		

Let us overview these four basic categories of perception. Technical data refer to a whole range of things we regard as fixed and factual. An example of technical data is "light bulbs give off light." Psychological information, on the other hand, refers to personal feelings and components of our consciousness that are "true" for us. Others, however, may not agree with us. Some examples of psychological information are: My girlfriend looks beautiful. All of my children are brilliant. This movie makes me sad.

The ego is a very special category; it is a collection of abstract thoughts and definitions we have about ourselves. The ego has increasingly played a more central role in many of our lives. A thought like "I am a good person" falls into this category.

Time data also deserves its own category—it is the most pervasive data we perceive. All our experiences, events, and memories are perceived by our Invisible Clock, and then assigned structure and significance by affixing a time. Experiences are recorded in a linear-dated sequence we see as a lifeline. Linear sequencing is particularly important because it's given an almost unchallengeable level of reliance in our thinking. ⧖

Once again, this particular categorization of perceptions has a unique purpose—to ultimately lead us to a better understanding of time. To make it perfectly clear, it is necessary to discuss the first three categories, technical data, psychological information, and the ego, before we move on to time data, which we will return to in the next chapter.

TECHNICAL DATA

If we look closely, we will see that even technical data—the information we usually consider to be absolutely factual—can be reliable or conditional. (Remember that technical data are a subset of all perceptions, which are, once again, incomplete, variable, and selective.) Factual information such as "keys open locks" and "water is wet", along with concepts such as proven mathematical formulas, are good examples of reliable technical data.

Conditional technical data also may be considered factual, yet they are subject to certain variables. Look at the statement "gold is valuable." Most people may believe this to be true. But what about for a cloistered monk living in a monastery? A person trapped on a deserted island? Gold simply doesn't have any absolute, intrinsic value. ⧗

We recognize these qualifying aspects of technical data immediately when they are pointed out. Otherwise, we tend to just accept them at face value. But, in order to think clearly, we need to become practiced and reflexive about identifying these factors in everyday life. Not nervously alert, just receptively aware of what is going through our minds.

> **Exercise 3.** Here are some technical statements that, under certain circumstances, may be relevant. Are these perceptions reliable or conditional? What qualifiers come to mind?
>
> - Water boils at 100 degrees centigrade.
> - The laws of gravity explain why objects are drawn to the earth's surface.
> - People buy things based on color.
> - A debit is never a credit to the same account.
> - Horses can be trained.

My own responses are the following: Number one is conditional; water boils at 100 degrees at sea level, but not on mountaintops. Its boiling point depends on atmospheric pressure. Number two is reliable. Nothing falls up, at least on earth. Three is reliably accurate only within specific parameters. The color of your car may be important to you, or maybe your dress, but probably not your toothpicks. Number four is reliable. It's an accepted convention for which accountants make no exceptions. (Notice the importance of the phrase "the same account.") Number five is also reliable; it is a true statement about the species in general. Maybe the horse you bought is as stubborn as a mule, but most horses are trainable.

The point here is that even facts may not be as factual as we at first believe. It is important, therefore, to not just accept them to be unconditionally true.

PSYCHOLOGICAL INFORMATION

Psychological data are thoughts and ideas we call emotions, beliefs, opinions, and attitudes—the perceptions that are accompanied by, or that easily arouse, feelings or sometimes even physical reactions.

We are so familiar with emotions that they hardly need to be defined. Fear, joy, and anger are common examples. Here is an example of an emotional stream of thought: I am angry with my boss. He never pays any attention to me. He doesn't appreciate me. I can't stand him.

Beliefs are a strong, complex structure through which we perceive the world, or ideas we hold with sincere confidence. Beliefs do not need to have immediate or well-defined proofs. Some examples are: I believe that hard work is its own reward. I believe that Elvis is still alive. I believe in ghosts. I believe that luck is more important than hard work. I believe in God.

Opinions are less dear to our hearts than beliefs. They are judgments about things we hold to be probably true, but fall short of absolute conviction or certainty. Opinions can be silly or serious, important or irrelevant. Some examples are: It's going to be a very cold winter with lots of snow. Interest rates are going to fall. My dog is the smartest dog on earth. Jazz is more creative than classical music. A missile defense program is necessary for the security of our nation.

Attitudes are dispositions or tendencies, or general frameworks of perception, perhaps more loosely defended and less crucial than beliefs but, nonetheless, intact rationales. Attitudes can predict our behavior with a high degree of probability. Some examples are: Once you fail, you're more likely to be a failure for life. There is another point of view, a "better" attitude: There are no failures, just opportunities to learn.

It is important to note that all psychological information is made up of the personal "feeling" components of our consciousness that are "true" for us. Not everyone may accept them to be true. But they nonetheless remain an integral part of our personal reality.

> **Exercise 4.** Using the words below, write a statement that expresses how you feel. Use only the psychological perception in brackets.
>
> - My mother (emotion)
> - Public school system (belief)
> - Work (attitude)
> - Chocolate (opinion)
> - Myself (belief)
> - Cats (emotion)
> - Tax rates which increase as income rises (opinion)
> - Possibility of failure (attitude)

Look at your responses. Imagine that someone else said these things to you. How would you interpret their statements? Are they positive or negative? What would you learn about the person from their answers?

This exercise brings us to a closer understanding of how our thoughts are structured by the interpretation of many thousands of our life's perceptions. Our mind's network of information is unique; no two people feel exactly the same way about these things. But the only way to clearly view our individual web of thoughts is to resist recklessly following the ones we might otherwise cherish or fear simply because they appear in our mind.

Here is another exercise in clear thinking.

Exercise 5. Take a few minutes to read the following statements. Are they technically true? Are they true only for you or also for others? Are they reliable or conditional statements? Are they psychological perceptions?

1. Fire is hot.
2. Keys open locks.
3. Snakes are disgusting.
4. Water is essential for life.
5. Fire is dangerous.
6. Feathers are light in weight.
7. Wood is heavy.
8. Compared to lead, wood is light.
9. It is rational to respect fire.
10. Some fires are hotter than others.

Here are my answers. Number one is technical and conditional. Fire can be hot, or not so hot. Burning alcohol is very cool compared to burning oak or metal. Statement two is technical and reliable. Keys are made to simply open and close locks. Number three is psychological. Snakes are just snakes whether you like them or not. But if you are looking for an assistant to work in the snake house at the zoo that psychological information becomes important technical data in the hiring process. ⧖

Four, six, and eight are technical and reliable. For number five, the immediate potential of danger with fire always exists, so the qualifier is important. Statement seven is technical and conditional since balsa wood is light. Nine is psychological and ten is a technical statement about conditional variables.

Clarity of vision comes when we consciously identify our psychological and technical perceptions, and do not confuse the two. Be careful of what you say to yourself. Be precise.

EGO

The ego is a subset of the data content of the mind, or the "who" in our store of memories. It is a very special category because it represents the self we are conscious of, and the many selves we have recorded in our memory in connection with personal events and relationships.

Who am I? Why am I here? These types of meaning-of-life questions are universal to all cultures. But they are questions we can never completely solve—indeed; there is no whole truth that can explain us completely. The practical answer to the question "Who am I?" depends on what we select from the vast storehouse of images and roles that we have in our minds.

Anyone who has stood in front of a display case filled with sunglasses and tried different lenses can imagine how the images and roles we choose to look through can change the world we see. Roles are technically very specific they describe who we are by the things we do, things such as being a: father, mother; son, daughter; employer, employee; cook, dieter; book reader, TV producer, couch potato, movie star, neighbor, friend or foe. They tend to change from situation to situation, person to person, and year to year. They even change throughout the day, and during a week it is possible to find ourselves in dozens of different roles.

Images are more psychological than technical. What do I really think of me? Images are descriptive and evaluative of ourselves in general or assessments of how well we perform our designated roles. I am honest, thin, handsome, a good person, a helpful parent, a kind friend, an impatient employer, a lazy employee, a stupid student, a genius? There is a seemingly infinite combination of images and roles in our minds data bank. The possibilities are endless.

Exercise 6. Take a few minutes to write some images and roles about yourself. Rank them in order of importance.

Now have a look at what you've written down. Ask yourself: How attached are you to these perceptions about yourself? Since they are perceptions, with the same limitations as other perceptions, are you absolutely certain of them? So certain that you feel you need not re-examine their validity?

What should we take away from this chapter? We have looked honestly at the wide variety of perceptions, yet all the time remaining aware that every perception is limited in its scope. For most people it is humbling to be reminded of how we actually perceive. No matter how we might want to believe what we think is "right," we must realize and admit our thoughts are perceptions and that all perceptions are, by definition, limited. To realize this is the first step to having an open mind, and eventually seeing time for what it really is.

Now, we are becoming more aware of the difference between technical data and psychological information. They are categories of perception that also form subcategories within many other categories. The distinction will become more apparent as we move towards a better understanding of our relationship with time.

We have begun to examine the role of the ego in our lives. Most people tend to regard their ideas about themselves as among the most sacrosanct that they have, and therefore the ones they hang on to with the tightest grip. But ego perceptions carry the same limitations as other perceptions. In later chapters we will discuss the difference between the ego and real identity.

Questions

1. Are you inclined to give more weight to the technical data you perceive or to the psychological information that "explains" it?

2. Do you often "wake up" in the middle of situations that you don't want to be in?

3. Do you think of yourself more in terms of the roles you play, the labels, such as mom, teacher, old man, your job title; or the things you do, the actions?

4. Are you a good listener? Or do spend a lot of time talking or thinking about yourself or other things?

5. Do you find yourself justifying the things you do by affirming that you've always been that way?

6. Do you find it difficult to think of your opinions and your self image as merely perceptions rather than facts?

Chapter 4

∞

TIME AS A PERCEPTION

*"It is easier to put up with unpleasantness from a
man of one's own way of thinking than from one
who takes an entirely different point of view."*

—*Napoleon I*

The past two chapters have overviewed the kinds of perceptions we have, and the limitations implicit in all of
them. The aim here is not to develop a cautious or anxious view of the impermanence of life. For although the
scope of perceptions may be limited, we can still be reasonably sure that, for example, the sun will come up

tomorrow. We must try to achieve a balance between what we believe to be true and the possibility that we could perhaps form a better understanding. To do this we must learn to be precise.

In this chapter, we will return to the examination of time that we each perceive with our own Invisible Clock. To reiterate, we cannot understand our relationship with time by seeing it as a phenomenon outside of ourselves. Remember, there are no tricks or shortcuts to understanding our perception of time. ⧖

Like other perceptions, our experience of time has similar limitations. As we discussed previously, time perceptions can be divided into three dimensions: experience, chronology, and circumstance. In this chapter we will consider the first of these, experience.

The following drawing illustrates how two different people experience and remember time.

Fig. 3: Mrs Smith and Laszlo on the train

Here is Mrs. Smith on her holiday tour traveling from
Austria to Hungary. She and Laszlo are taking the 7:02

express train from Vienna to Budapest. We can clearly see by their facial expressions and body language that their experience of this trip is quite different. Mrs. Smith seems annoyed by Laszlo and his smoking. Laszlo, on the other hand, looks happy and carefree.

The trip between these two cities takes about three hours. This is the technical data. For Mrs. Smith, it seems to take much longer. But for Laszlo, the trip is just routine. This describes their respective psychological experiences.

Why is this important? The interpretation of the event will not only affect how they feel about it now but also how they will remember it in the future. Mrs. Smith, for example, may decide that she will never travel to Budapest again even though she loves the city. For that matter, she may decide never to travel by train again. Her conclusion may seem irrational, but we make similar decisions all the time based on our perceptions of time and events stored in our memories. Our memories expend and spillover to interpret new events when we perceive them as being similar.

Time is personal, based on experience, and related to the events in our lives. It is a sense, not unlike other senses, that we perceive through our respective Invisible

Clocks. But of all our perceptual categories, time is the most difficult to see through. Even though we all experience time differently, the way each of us feels it seems so real, so absolute. And we are accustomed to discounting our own experience of time as invalid.

Let's break down the perception of time into its simplest components.

Table 3. Perception of Events in Time

Experience	Chronology	Circumstance
Technical	Dateline	Hierarchy of Impact
Psychological	Personal History	De-sequencing

The category of experience that appears in the top portion of the Time-Driven Mind (see *fig. 1,* page 6) provides the basic breakdown of how we interpret and input time data. As with most perceptions, there is a technical aspect and a psychological aspect. Technical time is simply measured time—a notation in terms of seconds, minutes, days, and years—while psychological time is our interpretation of that time, an editorial commentary that spills over to form the whole experience. Both are, nevertheless, perceptions.

It is the same process we observed in the example of the three-hour train ride from Vienna to Budapest. One word comparisons such as short versus long, fast versus slow, difficult or easy, uneventful or exciting come to mind. This editorial process enables us to make the jump from an evaluation about time, to an opinion about the event, that may both stem from our sense about the duration of time itself as well as other details of the event.

It is amazing how little consideration we give to our own experiences of time. As mentioned before, it is important not to dismiss our different experiences of time as mere tricks of the mind. Indeed, we should pay close attention to these differences. Examining these variations is crucial if we are to discover our real priorities and be able to control time the way we truly desire.

We have already reviewed several examples of the relativity of time that depends on individual viewpoints, but here are a few more points to consider.

What is the connection between the experience of time and age? How does time pass for a child waiting for Santa Claus compare to an adult's experience of Christmas Eve? How long does the average day seem for a five-year-old child? A twelve-year-old child? A senior citizen?

An overtaxed, busy parent? There seem to be many variations, although most of us assume that our experience is the "right" one. We should take the time to ask ourselves what perceptions led to these conclusions.

Another point to consider is the importance of culture in our experience of time. In many countries, words like "later" or "tomorrow" have completely different meanings than they do in the United States. Americans traveling to Europe, South America, or the Middle East may find themselves baffled by these changes in perception. In fact, in the West we may be offended when someone doesn't show up for an appointment at the scheduled time, whereas the original appointment may have been meant merely as a guideline to someone from another part of the world. ⧗

The essential lesson in all of this is that although we tend to regard time as absolute, we need to shake off any illusions of permanence we have about the sanctity of time kept by clocks and calendars.

Consider this. Watches are thought of as a great symbol of the absolute nature of time. But are they? After all, without the instrument on our wrist, we would often have no idea of the clock time. In fact, it is because of this subjective relativity that we need our watch in the first place! When we check our watches, should we not instead be reminded of our ability to become utterly consumed by our relative experiences of time?

It is an interesting irony that the clock, the most prominent symbol of time's "absolute" nature, may also be our greatest reminder of its relativity.

Questions

1. What sorts of things do you find yourself doing when you lose track of time?

2. What activities do you do that seem to drag on forever?

3. Whose company do you enjoy so much that when you speak to them you're not self conscious or worried about your image?

4. Do you often accuse others of being too slow or always in a rush?

5. Ask members of your family about a trip you've taken together. What was their experience of how time passed? How does it compare to yours?

6. Make a list of all the statements and excuses that you make about time. Some examples might be: I'm out of time. I'm late. If I only had the time.

Chapter 5

∞

DATELINES & PERSONAL HISTORIES

> *"Life is an offensive, directed against the repetitious mechanism of the Universe."*
> *—Alfred North Whitehead*

Our experience of time is a fascinating reality. On the one hand we have the technical data supplied by our clocks that allows us to coordinate from anywhere in the world. On the other hand we have our individual experience as interpreted by our Invisible Clock that is as unique to each of us as our own finger prints. Which begs the question: How do we see the world as a consequence of the way we experience time?

This chapter deals with how we store and sort all these experiences of time in what we will call our chronology. Our chronology deals, of course, with our past. Chronology can be understood best by considering it in two dimensions, our dateline and our personal history.

Dateline is the technical aspect of chronology. Some examples of dateline entries are: I was born on September 15, 1952; JFK was shot on November 22, 1963; I was married at 2 o'clock on August 18, 1975. Personal history data are the psychological information surrounding this chronology. Some examples of personal history are: We've been married over 25 years, and we still feel like newlyweds. I can't believe I'm almost fifty. Those ten years we've lived in this house passed so quickly. ⧗

Our attachment to what we experience as a comforting certainty of clock time translates into an overwhelming fixation on both chronological aspects of our consciousness, our datelines and personal histories. They structure our thinking, and as we will see in the next chapter, we manipulate them as well. Let us read through the story of Rachel. It will demonstrate how pervasive these elements are in our lives.

My name is Rachel, and I was born on October 20, 1960. My mom was in her early forties when she had me. That was kind of uncommon in the 1960s. Before I was four years old she began to teach me how to read. She was ambitious; she always wanted me to be ahead of my age group. When I got to kindergarten, I managed to skip a grade. I was only five when I started first grade. Otherwise I had a pretty normal life until I was nine. That's when my dad died. I'll never forget the date: June 3rd. It was only a few days before my parent's fifteenth wedding anniversary. It took mom a couple of years to get over it. Some of her friends said she was taking too long, that she should start dating again, but she said she needed more time. To overcome her grief, she took some piano lessons. Her mother told her that pushing fifty was no time to be taking up the piano. In fact, she had a hard time finding a teacher. But mom told me that after she suddenly lost dad, she had the feeling that life was short. She knew that she should do what she wanted no matter what anybody else thought.

I was glad she took lessons three times a week, because she used to take me with her and I could play with the instructor's cute son, David. We became good friends, and in our senior year we began dating. We went to the prom together, and afterwards I lost my virginity. June 21! I remember I colored in that date on my calendar, and mom asked me what it was for. I told her it was my friend's birthday! Now I always buy a rose on that day each year, just to mark the day and remember. I wonder what David's doing now. I hear he has two kids, three and six, and is on his second marriage. Sometimes I wonder what would have happened if we had stayed together. Even though I'm too old for those kind of fantasies!

What should we take away from this example? Even though this is a fairly succinct, average description of a woman's early life, there are an overwhelming number of dates, ages, birthdays, references to the decade or year, and anniversaries. In fact, this time-oriented chronology forms the backbone of Rachel's self history. This keel of her mind's ship—her official version of the "facts"—is the foundation of her conscious mind.

How does this work? The technical organization of events as we remember them is collected in a unidirectional sequence by day, date, and time. It is our recollection of a lifetime of experience arranged in a conventional and measured order. We cling to these dates and times, and they give us a safety blanket when clear memories of the events fade into the distance.

Our dateline is accompanied by a personal history, or the psychological interpretation of these events. This is the story that we tell ourselves and others about ourselves, the story that we believe is factually and unequivocally supported by the dateline. We rely on our datelines and personal history for the continuity and confirmation of who we are.

As we can see from Rachel's example, a lot of weight is given to these chronological measurements. She is always aware of how old she is when certain things happened to her. You can also see how much chronological age factors into her and family's decision-making process. She tells us how her mother wanted her to be "ahead" of other kids her age, rather than simply accomplished at a certain task. Rachel's mom is expected to grieve at a cer-

tain pace, whether she is ready to or not, and is not supposed to take piano lessons after a certain age because she
is thought to be too old. Rachel herself feels too old to
fantasize about an old lover.

Clearly we impose many limitations on ourselves
based on time. Our self-imposed restrictions can range
from silly, like we shouldn't wear white after Labor Day, to
serious; like we are too old to do something we really want
to do. We expect our children to reach levels of profi-
ciency relative to their ages, and we are very disappointed
if they don't. We expect ourselves to be making a certain
amount of money within a certain timeframe, and if we
don't, we feel as though we are not succeeding as we
would like.

We cannot change our experience of time. But we can
change how much significance we attach to our datelines
and personal histories. Both are inevitable aspects of
being human. But sometimes we attach importance to the
"reality" of dates and times and thoughtlessly conclude
that the story of our past encapsulates who we are and
where we imagine we want to go.

Exercise 7a. Organize ten important events from your

lifetime in chronological sequence. Record only the first
ten that come to mind, without editing your choices.
Here are some suggestions: taking your driver's test,
high school graduation, marriage, birth of a child, getting
your first kiss, a dangerous escape. Then after each
event, list the date when it happened, how old you were
when it happened, and briefly outline the significance of
each event.

Take a look at your answers. Ask yourself the following
questions. Why did I choose these events? Would I have
chosen differently yesterday?

Exercise 7b. Now list five events in your life that you
consider to be positive achievements. (They do not have
to be life-changing events.) List five more events that you
consider to be unfortunate mistakes. (They do not have
to be disasters.) Try to place all of these in the chronological dateline you listed above.

Compare your answers to 7a with 7b. Then ask yourself,
which ones have the most impact on my life, the positive
or the negative? You will notice that there might be some
events that you consider to be milestones, even though

nothing of significance really happened in the "real" world outside yourself. There are probably events that you consider to be quite significant that you cannot place with absolute certainty in your official chronology. Even though we know it is unreliable and contains errors, we still depend on our "official" chronology as the impeccable proof that the things in it really happened just the way we remember them.

Take a moment to consider that there used to be no clocks and no calendars. How was life different then? Many people didn't know their birthdays, they didn't celebrate Mother's Day, they didn't even know the time of day, and they certainly didn't know the year. In other words, time did not measure out every detail of our lives, providing a stick by which to evaluate our "progress". How much do all of these dates and memories in time really contribute to our lives? ⧗

There are two larger lessons underlying Rachel's example. The first is that our datelines and personal histories can become so central to us that we look at them as "who we are." The nature of perceptions is such that the first thing we think of when faced with a new situation is how we remember handling a similar situation in the past.

How does this influence our dealings with the present? For one thing, if we are only thinking in the past, we can't be examining the current situation with fresh eyes. So we are probably going to do what we think has worked for us in the past rather than being open to possibly improving or changing. Instead of expecting and embracing the new circumstances, we are disoriented when the present seems to conflict with our past. We even have the tendency to rewrite history so that we don't have to live with those uncomfortable conflicts and discrepancies that may challenge the past because they do not run parallel to our present. There is more to come about this point in the next chapter.

Perhaps the most significant consequence of the importance we attach to our datelines and personal histories is that we tend to regard what we are experiencing in the present as simply a notch in our dateline, the next entry in the continuing expanse of our history. The present, then, tends to loose its significance next to the sum total of our past. Of course, to view the experience of time this way makes it very difficult to focus on living in the present. There will also be more about this in the following chapters.

Questions

1. Recall a childhood memory. Now try and remember what you were doing last Thursday at 2 p.m. Which memory is more immediate?

2. How often do you think about how old you are? How often do you wish you were younger? Older? At some optimum age?

3. What kinds of things would you be doing if you were the age you wish you were? What are the limitations implicit in these endeavors that make them impossible to do now?

4. When asked to describe who you are, do you immediately avoid or include your age? Do you focus on what you've done in the past?

5. Do you think your best days are over? Waiting for you after retirement?

6. Do you usually wake up excited to begin a new day? Do you ever dread the day ahead?

7. How did you define "old" when you were ten? When you were twenty? At the age you are now?

Chapter 6

∞

HIERARCHY OF IMPACT
& DE-SEQUENCING

Do I contradict myself?
Very well then I contradict myself,
(I am large, I contain multitudes.)
                              —*Walt Whitman*

The last chapter dealt with how we store and organize time data that we've already experienced into a chronology. In this chapter we will see how we use this chronology to color our current circumstances—how the web of both our datelines and personal histories affect our view of what is happening right now. Take a moment and refer once again to *figure 1* (page 6), the Time-Driven Mind.

Examples in the previous chapter illustrate how obsessed we have become with the dates and times that we think collectively define who we are. As a rule, we draw no distinction between our identity and what we remember from our past. In fact, our history is often interpreted as our entire identity. The present, then, becomes nothing more than a logical extension of a linear, unswerving sequence that is our life. It is nothing but a small dot on the landscape of our dateline.

Yet as we all know, we do not actually experience the present that way. We cannot exist in the past, nor can the past reappear in the present. Every day we are faced with new circumstances—those "external" events happening in the world around us right now. They change in a non-linear and unpredictable way. Every day is a new day, every instant a new instant, and nobody knows what will happen next. So what tricks do our minds play on us to create the illusion that the past is still present?

The two most common modes of thinking we use to manipulate our perception of our current circumstance are called hierarchy of impact and de-sequencing. Hierarchy of impact describes how dominant memories overshadow other memories from our past, along with our current perceptions. De-sequencing, on the other hand, is an alteration of our standard chronology. An example of this is the process of selecting memories out of sequence with no regard for dates and times to support our current view. The irony is that the chronological structure of our memory is what provides us with the legitimacy we depend on in recalling events in the first place. Yet when we engage in de-sequencing, we totally ignore the chronology and extract data as required from wherever we need in order to reinforce our opinions about our current circumstance.

Let us further examine how these phenomena work.

HIERARCHY OF IMPACT

Most of us tend to define ourselves through our past, projecting our storylines and datelines like a filter over our current situation, regardless of whether it is appropriate or not. One of the most obvious ways we do this is through the phenomenon we call hierarchy of impact. But its impact is not always an earth-shattering identity crisis;

it can be a simple matter of taste. Let us consider Jason's predicament.

> Five years ago, Jason came down with the flu after eating a big piece of chocolate cake. It used to be his favorite dessert, but he has not eaten a slice since. His girlfriend has just baked him a chocolate cake for his birthday. She pulls it out of the oven, and it smells heavenly. Will Jason eat the cake?

Jason's unfortunate experience with chocolate cake forms a very predictable outcome according to our definition of hierarchy of impact. It is like the summit of a mountain casting a shadow on everything below it. Jason finds it very difficult to eat the cake, even though he himself may think that his reason for doing so is kind of silly. Nevertheless, he knows his past—he can't or won't forget that he felt sick after he ate cake, and this experience overwhelms his present vision.

If we believe that we are no more than the sum of our past datelines and personal histories, then we can't escape an unhealthy attachment to our inaccurate and incomplete memories. Remember, our datelines and histories suffer from the same restrictions as other perceptions—they are incomplete, variable, and selective. Nonetheless, we manage to find ways to remain loyal to our past experiences in order to feel secure, even if they are not logically related to our current circumstance, and even if they will hurt us in the long run. Whether intentional or not, we see what is going on around us through a prism of the past. It clouds our ability to see clearly right now. Just like Jason, we don't eat the chocolate cake when we could.

Jason's example is valuable not only because it illustrates an immediate reliance on a dominant experience, but also shows how irrational the process can be. Logically speaking, Jason knows that a piece of cake was not likely related to having the flu. Yet that negative experience from five years ago exerts an oddly powerful pull. In other words, the dominant memory that is at the root of his experience acts like the first of many dominos, affecting all others in its path. It is the most relevant experience he has, even if it is not very closely related to his present reality. So instead of looking at his new experience by separating the technical from the psychological, trying hard to overcome his prejudices to see as clearly as possible, he succumbs to the most powerful past experience he has, and lives with it.

Imagine how the following experiences would affect how you view the past or present.

1. A divorce

2. A shark bite

3. Graduating first in your class

4. A car accident

5. Food poisoning

6. Being searched at an airport

7. Being audited

8. Getting stuck overnight in an elevator

9. Meeting Nelson Mandela

Let us take a look at the first example. Imagine that you had a very ugly divorce, and that it figures very high on the hierarchy of memories that have had the most impact on your life. Remarkably, in addition to perhaps souring your view of the future possibilities of marriage, it spurs you to re-write your own history. It affects the way you now view your entire marriage. Although you may have been blissful in the beginning, now you can imagine yourself saying "we were never that happy" or "I had a feeling it wasn't going to last." Would you see your wedding photographs in the same way as you did when you were happily married? Could you find yourself agreeing with statements like "marriage is a defunct institution" or "men (or women) can never be trusted"? To summarize, in this case a hierarchy of impact is created by an overwhelming event (the divorce) that spurs you to change your personal history in order to match your current world view. ⧗

DE-SEQUENCING

In the same way dominant past experiences affect our past and present in a hierarchy of impact, changing the official memory and order of our chronology to meet our current needs is a process called de-sequencing. Let us look at the following example.

Linda has had the same hairstyle for the past fifteen years. She remembers it as ten, but it was actually fifteen. About the time Linda got it she received many compliments, and it still looks good to her. She hates to change her hairstyle because once, when she was a kid, she got a terrible perm that resulted in her being teased for months. But she knows the hairstyle is out-of-date, and a friend she trusts has told her that she needs a change. Will Linda cut her hair?

Notice how in this example Linda has conveniently forgotten dates, yet the error is in favor of the decision she wants to make. She has de-sequenced the facts; her memory of events surrounding her hairstyle has changed. Somehow she's let the crucial fact slip her mind so that now she thinks it's only been ten years since her last hairstyle change. In truth, she doesn't like the thought of getting a new hairstyle, and having the same style for ten years isn't as bad as fifteen.

In effect, she has selected supporting events from everywhere in her chronology without regard for the order in which they occurred. Why? Her de-sequencing process clearly helps her rationalize her current desires. Since she doesn't want to face the facts, she delves into the murky past and re-orders it to match the decision she desires.

This example also illustrates a hierarchy of impact, in this case the teasing surrounding her childhood hairstyle. This explains her general hesitation to change her hair.

De-sequencing and hierarchy of impact illustrate very clearly what happens if instead of looking anew at current circumstances we project our past to judge our situation right now. If our past is like a piece of software that makes our decisions, we must continually be fiddling with it to meet our ever-changing reality. In truth, this is an exhausting way to live. We re-write and tamper with our own histories, and each time we know deep down that we're kidding ourselves.

The truth is that it is much easier and more accurate to simply consider the technical and psychological data, like whether we like chocolate cake or need a haircut. Since the world does not unravel in a predictable, knowable, absolute manner, we must not be content with the conditioned comfort of the past. The best indicator of our present is the present. But so often we cling to the past and try to make it fit, or become overpowered by it by not attempting to clearly see beyond it. If we are determined to see the present through the past, how can we avoid making the same mistakes? How can we be excited about what's going on around us?

WHY YOU ARE NOT YOUR PAST AND NOT YOUR EGO

Many, if not most, people do not challenge the belief that their past equals their identity, that they are nothing more than what they remember. Who you are is a collection of everything you've done, everything you've seen, everyone you've known, everything you've experienced, and everything you think about yourself. The sum total of all of these things, many believe, is that person's identity, who they think they are as human beings.

The past does play a very big role in our consciousness. Storing information is obviously an integral part of the mind's natural function. No one would want to wake up every day with amnesia; it would be impossible to function normally. And even if we thought it would be a good idea to get rid of our past, as some people no doubt desire, how would we do it? We are constantly bombarded by memories. We may be sitting on our couch and, for no reason, suddenly we think about a childhood pet, our most enjoyable vacation, people who mean a lot to us who we may not have seen for a while, loved ones who have passed on, the way the trees looked in the backyard of our first home. When people lose their homes to fire they most often regret the loss of their photographs. Our memories are some of the most valuable treasures we possess. No one should dispute that.

Our memories can have such a powerful pull on us that sometimes we forget that they are not who we are. We are more than the sum of our parts, including our memories. Sometimes, of course, it is a good idea to reflect on our past, but we must be aware that when we do this we are not focused on the present but lost in our minds.

The most important revelation about the past stems from the realization that it is not important to try and get rid of it, but to realize that we are already, by definition, rid of it. We need not be convinced of the importance of living in the present, but instead realize that we inevitably live in the present, and the only thing to do is to face it. Many times our past seems so immediate to us that it is like it never left us. Sometimes it seems so meaningful and precious that we want to hold on to it. Or like Newton, we imagine that our present is simply an extension of the past. But, like for Newton, the error comes from an incorrect assumption about time. It is a fact that the past is gone, and two seconds ago is equally as gone as two millennia ago. Now is not just a speck on our dateline. Even if we are thinking about the past, we are doing it now.

Whether we like it or not, we cannot escape the present. The only reality is now. This, in fact, is the central principle of the Mission-Driven Mind (see *fig. 2* page 7), which we will begin to focus on in the next chapter.

If the only reality is now, then our identity must also exist completely in the now. Who we are is who we are right now. One of the unfortunate legacies of the past century was the assumption that we need to conclusively define and label who we are. But an accurate definition of the self is impossible. You are more than you realize, more than you can define. And the more time you spend trying to nail down the definition, the less time you spend living right now. You cannot be thinking about you and concentrating on whatever is before you at the same time. Your past is not your identity, and your ego is not your identity. You, living now, is your identity.

Questions

1. When you approach a new circumstance, do you immediately try to remember how you handled a similar circumstance in the past rather than try to learn all you can about the present situation?

2. At work, would you rather stick to things you already know than try something new?

3. Make a list of some of the most influential experiences of your life. How do you think each experience changed how you felt about other aspects of your life? Did you feel more positive after the experience? Negative? Doubtful? Fearful?

4. How often do you find yourself more interested in reveling in the past rather than living right now?

5. Do you like to dream about the future? Does it make you feel better about the present?

6. Do you think that the more rigid the definition, the more clearly you know yourself?

7. When is the last time you did something that surprised even you? Was it a pleasant or frightening experience?

8. Do you become fearful when you don't follow a routine?

9. Do you fear that if you don't make yourself think good things about your past you will forget the people you love?

10. Do you fear that if you don't remind yourself often of past mistakes you won't be a successful person?

Chapter 7

ONE PRIORITY AT A TIME

*"If they want we will give them a sleeping bag,
but there is something romantic about sleeping
under the desk. They want to do it."*

—*Bill Gates,*

on his young software programmers.

The previous three chapters have dealt with the three perceptual components of the Time-Driven Mind as illustrated by the entire top of the hourglass pictured in *figure 1* (see page 6). We have overviewed in detail how we experience, store, and sort time, and how it comes to bear on our present circumstances. Clearly our assumptions about the absolute nature of time have permeated every aspect of our lives. As a rule, we discount our immediate experience in favor of our obsession with calendars, dates, and ages, constantly fighting the losing battle of trying to harmonize our emerging present with commentaries from the past.

If we see time though this model there are certain inevitable consequences. Referring again to *figure 1*, we have depicted the process of how experience, chronology, and our interpretation of current circumstance are all projected through the expedient of measured time. We will now begin to see how this view of time has a direct impact on how we decide on our priorities, establish a sense of urgency to go along with our "priorities", and how that affects our ability to coordinate our activities.

Take a look at *figure 2* (page 7) which illustrates the Mission-Driven Mind. The bottom half of the Time-Driven Mind and the Mission-Driven Mind deal, in fact, with the same three topics. While the Time-Driven Mind has multiple priorities, a swinging pendulum of various levels of urgency, and coordination based on the demands of clock time, the Mission-Driven Mind replaces these elements with one priority, a feeling of inspiration, and the ability to really synchronize with others. Working our way through the next three chapters we will see how to translate the first model into the second. We begin by looking at priorities. ⧗

If we see time as merely a clock on the wall, we decide on our priorities based on what we think we have time to do given the hours, days, and weeks ahead. Since what we are doing now is simply a small speck on the expanse of our dateline, we might feel that it is not important to do anything. Instead we might choose to plan our future, preferably as far ahead as possible. Not surprisingly, we assume that we've succeeded when we wind up with many detailed priorities. But let us look at a typical description of priorities someone might have over the span of a week. Let's call this Ms. B's plan.

> This week I want to get my resume in order and start looking for a new job. I want to spend some quality time with my little girl, and take my husband out to dinner. I want to pick up the drycleaning and buy a new teapot. I want to finish reading the novel I started six months ago.

Exercise 8. This is a good opportunity to see just how this works for all of us. Take a few minutes to make a list of the priorities you see as important for you to work on during the coming week.

Now that we have done that, let's return to Ms. B. What do you notice about her plans? First of all, her priorities range from the most important things she can do with her time, like changing jobs, to the most mundane, like buying a teapot. Closer scrutiny reveals that she likely has a rushed and scattered life. She has to pencil in "quality time" with her husband and little girl. She seems to feel somewhat guilty about the fact that she started a novel six months ago and still hasn't finished it.

Now we can ask ourselves this important question: Does my list have the same characteristics as Ms. B's?

The underlying assumption in Ms. B's planning is, of course, Newtonian—that time unfolds in a linear and uni-directional manner and that the following week will pass like an arrow traveling at a uniform and predictable speed for a foreseeable future. And, therefore, to handle these uniform and predictable chunks of time—each speck of now being just as important or significant as all the other theoretical specks in our future—all we must do is to plan in advance. Ms. B is seeing time as illustrated in the Time-Driven Mind (page 6).

Let us compare this example with another person, one who has just had a personal crisis that immediately brought his world into focus and who functions in accordance with the Mission-Driven Mind (page 7). We'll call him Mr. M.

What am I going to do in the next week? Well, after I nearly died in a car crash, I look at life differently. I've gained a new focus and seriousness for the work that I am doing. So I keep my scheduling to a minimum and concentrate on what I can do now to complete the goals I have set for myself. I have the will and the courage to see what important people and circumstances are in my life now. So it may be that as an architect I need to complete the office design for my client and, therefore, I open the computer file and begin. It may, however, be more important to call a friend who needs me. I now have the clarity and focus to know the difference. Frankly, I used to be scared of letting go of rigid scheduling. But now I like it. I feel alive and invigorated with the possibilities in each moment. Not to mention I am more productive than ever.

In the first example, Ms. B is projecting what she thinks she wants to do based on past experiences through a prism of measured time. She comes up with a lot of priorities that she has no interest in doing at that exact moment, but presumes she will want to do in some theoretical moment in the future.

In the second example, on the other hand, Mr. M is focused on what he needs to do right now. He is driven by a sense of mission rather than clock time. He understands his life goals along with what he can and cannot do about them today. Focusing on now enhances his ability to accomplish them because it always takes into account the new and current circumstance that he knows can change in an instant. The right priority replaces a list of priorities in a calendar book on his desk. He never lets himself forget that all he has is the present. It is no longer a speck on his dateline, it is everything. He is a Mission-Driven person.

Most of us think having a list of priorities is a sign of a motivated, serious person. But there is one essential flaw in this perspective. We are not guaranteed a future; and even if we were we could not live in it. All we have is now. If we are living in the present moment, there is only room for one priority. Only one is possible at a time. Otherwise we are distracted or second guessing ourselves, wondering if we should be doing what we are doing. It is impossible to have multiple priorities and to focus our attention exclusively. It's only logical that we can only give one hundred percent of our attention to one thing at a time. Otherwise it would not be, by definition, our full attention.

Most very successful people are just like the Microsoft employees that Bill Gates refers to in the quotation at the beginning of this chapter. They are focused on one priority. People naturally focus on one priority when they are doing something they love. Clock time and lists of priorities lose their significance when we are absorbed in what we enjoy, in this case, programming software. These employees were naturally living in the now as a consequence of their enthusiasm. But to do this with any degree of consistency, it is important for most of us to develop a deeper understanding of our relationship with time.

Of course our priority can and will change when we know it is appropriate. We can, for example, read the newspaper, and not be distracted by someone else entering the room. Or we can change our focus to that person and stop reading the newspaper.

But we cannot predetermine a formula that usurps our vision and our will any more than we can schedule our life down to the smallest detail and expect success. Schedules also act as cushions for us, rationalizations on why we are not doing what we want to do. They contribute to the process of looking away from the present.

We all have long-term goals—wanting to own a house, for example. But for every goal there is an action we can take right now. There is only one moment to live, now. And for every now there is one best action.

It does take courage to stop living in some theoretical future or distorted past and to just exist without all the regular excuses. It may feel disorienting or uncertain. It may even feel raw. In some ways it can be compared to looking into the eyes of a very direct person. There might be a tendency to at first look away even though there may be no valid reason to do so. Naturally this kind of discipline doesn't come easy nor will it be accomplished overnight.

Besides courage, it also takes practice. To be aware of the distinction between time-based priorities and one real priority requires a trained mind. Time-based priorities are conditional; we can change them whenever we like. They are filtered though all the levels of perception as we reconstruct and project them. By contrast, one mission-driven priority requires that we understand the true nature of our Invisible Clock and the way we actually perceive time. We must accept that all we have is now, and the best way to deal with now is to bring all our attention to it and focus entirely on it.

Ask yourself this question. What is my one priority, right now? The answer is the same for all of us—reading this book! If this is not your priority why are you doing this now?

Questions

1. Do you make resolutions each New Year's? On your birthday? How many of these resolutions do you actually carry out?

2. When you list priorities, are they simple tasks, like grocery lists, or broader, like asking yourself what life changes you need to make?

3. When you are trying to figure out which priority to do first, by what criteria do you judge? Do you put oth-

ers' needs before your own? Do you have a hard time deciding?

4. Are you very often disappointed in yourself for not carrying out all your priorities?

5. Do you try and please everybody, and secretly feel resentful that no one notices?

6. Are you continually changing your mind about what you want to do?

7. How many of your priorities would still be important if you knew your days were numbered?

8. Do you think you are good at staying focused on one thing at a time, or are you easily distracted?

9. Are you afraid of finding out who you really are, or what you really want to do with your life? If so, why?

Chapter 8

∞

PANIC, APATHY, INSPIRATION

To see a world in a grain of sand
And heaven in a wild flower,
Hold infinity in the palm of your hand
And eternity in an hour.

—*William Blake*

The last chapter outlined how we should move away from keeping long, unwieldy lists of priorities that allow no room to see the current circumstance clearly. We must also be aware that it is the nature of perceptions that what we see is constantly changing, and our reaction to it will constantly be renewed. Our clearest vision can only come from what we see and do right now.

In this chapter we will discuss how our assumptions about time affect our sense of urgency about the things we have to do. Urgency is defined here as the psychological response to things we choose to do, or the energy we bring to a situation. When it is projected through measured time, the levels of urgency vary over a broad spectrum. We will compare an example illustrating this mode of operating to another that encapsulates the Mission-Driven Mind. Our ultimate goal here is to understand how to reach a consistent state of inspiration, defined as both an idea and the feeling we get when we know that our direction is the right one.

Table 4: Levels of Urgency

0	**Apathetic**	I don't care
1	**Uncertain**	I'm not confident
2	**Attentive**	I'm aware of its importance
3	**Dutiful**	I'm convinced that this is what I must do now
4	**Anxious**	I'm distracted
5	**Nervous**	I'm very worried
6	**Panicked**	I'm out of control

Let us have a look at what Ms. B wrote when she addressed what she feels about the list of priorities she outlined in the last chapter.

> It's pretty important for me to get my resume done, but I'm kind of nervous about it. I should have done it weeks ago. When it comes to spending time with my husband and daughter, I guess I would rank my level of urgency as dutiful. I'm apathetic about picking up the dry-cleaning, and since the teapot is a gift I'm anxious I'll forget. I'm uncertain about finishing the novel. It's been so long now I'm not confident I'll ever finish it.

Exercise 9. Refer to the list of priorities you wrote for the last chapter and similarly attach a level of urgency to each one.

Ms. B's description contains a bewildering variety of feelings, ranging from apathetic to very worried. But we should not blame her for feeling overwhelmed by choices. After all, where is her gauge? Now, take a look at your own description. Are your levels of urgency comparable? What do you really want to do now?

Exercise 10. Look at your list of priorities again. How would your priorities change if a close family member became sick? You were offered a promotion within your company? You had a car accident? Your spouse said you were too fat?

There is something about a crisis that forces us to focus on one priority. But why don't we do this consistently? Why don't we see and appreciate the opportunity we have every moment of every day? Where is our sense of mission in life?

Now read what Mr. M, who, you'll remember, is living in accordance with the model of the Mission-Driven Mind, wrote about his priorities.

Well, since I haven't listed off a bunch of priorities, it's hard to imagine how I would feel about them. I find that when you live in the present moment, you somehow know what you want to do right now. When you're inspired to do something, that sense is built in. Each person is different, and each second is different. You can't predict what's coming. But you always know what needs to be done right now. There is one compelling thing for every second if you look at it honestly.

Notice in the above description that the man is acting on only one level, that of inspiration, the irresistible force to take the right action right now. Living in the now has allowed him to escape the oscillating pendulum that swings from apathy and panic. He devotes his attention to each individual moment, does the thing that needs to be done, and feels inspired doing it.

Take a moment to once again contrast the Mission-Driven Mind (page 7) model to the Time-Driven Mind (page 6) model. See the simplicity and elegance in the Mission-Driven model. There is one right priority and one level of urgency, that of inspiration. It truly is the sweet spot of the mind.

It is important to note here that living each moment is not the same as doing the first spontaneous thing that comes into your mind. This is not a matter of "if it feels good, do it." Quite the contrary. In separating the technical from the psychological, in watching our thoughts, and in finding true priorities, our rational abilities and goals are enhanced and clarified. For example, maybe what you want to do right now is apply to medical school. Ask yourself: Is this a passing fad, or is it something you believe you will be excited about when you get up every morning for the rest of your life? Is it your passion? Or are you doing it only because you want a "good" career? Because it is your parents' dream? Big decisions must be considered, but the right decision will become clear if our attention stays in the present, and away from the distortions of the past or projection of the future. There will be more about this in following chapters. ⏳

Of course, we do not relinquish all the chores of life just by living in the now. But isn't it much more likely that even mundane necessities will be more appealing if we act purposefully? Imagine that you are going to the grocery store, and you are focused on what you are doing rather than lost in some reverie far away. Maybe you will notice the look on someone's face, and derive pleasure from it. Maybe the banks of sparkling vegetables will look better to you than they did rushing past in a frenzy. There can be a sense of peace and curiosity from living each moment, no matter what you happen to be doing.

People who have had a recent brush with death or those who are more enlightened do not act hastily or imprudently, even if they do stop and smell the roses. Living in present should never be confused with an exercise in moral relativism. People who live in the present generally are not the ones who selfishly fulfill their own whims. On the contrary, they tend to be much more aware of how their actions affect others. Their eyes are wide open to the consequences of their actions.

Time as we experience it exists as one now at a time. Our now is our consciousness and our compass. Without it we are lost in a maze of competing needs and desires. We try to find our way, puzzling though various systems of abstract moralities, trying to please everyone else and ourselves, but we ignore the most important gauge we have: Our mind open to inspiration. When we start to feel panicky or apathetic, we need to take a breath and return ourselves to the present. We need to see our Invisible Clock and observe its movement in our thoughts. We must recognize that only we can bring the important people and events in our lives together in harmony.

Questions

1. Have you resigned yourself to feeling apathetic? Panicky? Do you think you must feel like that, or can you consider that it is a perception that can be changed?

2. When you feel bored with something, do you stop to consider why?

3. When you feel panicky, do you stop to consider why?

4. Do you do or say things when you're upset and blame it on the clock?

5. Do you blame others, or life in general, when you're bored with what you're doing?

6. Do you think that only lucky people feel inspired?

7. What were you doing the last time you felt inspired?

8. Do you find it impossible to derive any pleasure from so-called "unimportant" things like driving, shopping, or watering plants?

9. Do you try to do the right thing most of the time? Or do you just try and please yourself?

10. Do you find yourself acting on whims? Do you live with a lot of regret about your actions?

11. Do you often wish you were doing something else, with someone else, somewhere else?

Chapter 9

COORDINATION VS. SYNCHRONIZATION

"In preparing for battle I have always found that
plans are useless, but planning is indispensable."
—*Dwight D. Eisenhower*

Let us review what we've learned in the previous two chapters. It's possible that our assumptions about the infallibility of measured time have taken us down a path of uncertainty. We are not totally sure of what we need to do at any given moment. We have become distracted, ordered about by the perceived demands of measured time. We focus and refocus on many priorities with little regard for which one we should complete first. We find ourselves vacillating between panic and boredom, and inspiration comes seldom and randomly. In the worst case, we have turned away from our present, and, in doing so, we have turned away from ourselves.

In this chapter we will see how this same dynamic directly interferes with our ability to communicate and work effectively with others. We will look at the distinction between coordination, or meeting for meeting's sake, and synchronization, or the process of being aware of our own Invisible Clock while respecting and seeking to understand its dynamics in others. As in the past two chapters, we will look at this comparison in relation to the Time-Driven (page 6) and Mission-Driven Mind (page 7) models.

Coordination is the perception of being in harmony with the important people and events in our lives. In today's world, the primary consideration when arranging a meeting of any kind is clock time. When people want to coordinate, the first thing they do is check their calendars or watches. But should it be the first and sometimes only consideration?

The ability to coordinate is one of the main reasons clocks and calendars were invented in the first place. Of course no one would dispute the utility of clock time for this end—it is certainly more precise to say meet me for lunch at 1:00 p.m. rather than when the sun is directly above the main square. But, as we all know, meeting is a lot more than converging at the same geographical location.

Let us have a look at the following example of how the Time-Driven Mind attempts coordination with others.

> The manager of XYZ Corp. has called a meeting for 10:00 a.m. on Tuesday to discuss a new project which will produce the revenues to meet the company's third-quarter projections. He is eager to complete the project because it will eventually lead to his quarterly bonus. So he gathers seven employees who will work on this project for a meeting.
>
> All employees arrive within five minutes of the set time, perhaps aware of the meeting agenda, but also with their own set of individual priorities. Employee one is looking for a raise which he has decided he must have or he will take another

job he has been offered. Employee two wants a promotion so is interested in pleasing the boss and will work hard on the project. Employee three is going to take tomorrow off and is thinking about what she needs to do. Employee four is just here for the paycheck. Employee five finds the project interesting and is ready to start. Employee six has a big date for lunch and is thinking of nothing else. Employee seven wants to make a name for himself and will challenge anything his manager says.

The manager has succeeded in coordinating all of the employees. That is, they all showed up for the meeting at the correct time. But will he be successful in completing his project? Unfortunately, without each individual realizing the importance of the current priority, or having the present vision to see the basis of a shared priority, it may or may not work. Unless the manager can change his employees' perceptions and unify their vision, the results will be very unpredictable. This is the result of working with others according to the Time-Driven Mind model.

How would this work if the manager was working according to the model of the Mission-Driven Mind? To move toward the goal of synchronization, the manager first needs to be aware of and understand his own Invisible Clock. He needs to ask the question, what is my priority? Is my focus on completing this project for the customer, or on the bonus? Is my role of being the boss more important than getting the job done? Do I feel inspired or just anxious about completing the task? ⏳

As he understands his own priority and sense of urgency he can then effectively focus on the Invisible Clocks of others. This is where real leadership comes into play. Understanding others' Invisible Clocks requires intelligence and attention. The manager needs to look at his employees carefully and discover their priorities and sense of urgency. Who was paying attention at the meeting? Who asked relevant questions? Who was staring at the ceiling or looking at his watch?

Synchronization is a true meeting of minds focused on one recognized priority. It is only possible when we are taking the right action with the right people for the right reasons and at the only time we have, now.

Once again, let us take a look at Mr. M, who has awakened to his own potential and, as we have seen, has a Mission-Driven perspective.

> When I agree to meet with a new client I spend most of the time listening. I stay attuned to things that are important to them, their opinions and attitudes. I ask myself, why are they telling me this now? Do they have negative or positive expectations? Are they inspired to take action now or are they just feeling out the possibilities? What is their priority? And, ultimately, can I join them in their vision? It is amazing how little I used to listen, and how much more I hear now. People's opinions and creative insight continue to amaze me. By learning as much as I can about them, I can determine if we can focus on a shared priority and, in turn, create something new that all of us can feel excited about and proud of.

Mr. M has transcended the idea of mere coordination and, since he is focused on one priority at a time, one client at a time, he consequently aims for a meeting of the minds, for true synchronization. He pays close attention to others and looks for their Invisible Clocks as well as his own.

Of course this principle applies just as well to our private lives as to our professional lives. It is impossible to relate well to others without respecting both your Invisible Clock and theirs. Do not assume you know what others are thinking or feeling. Even if you know them well, they change every day, just like you do. Listen as carefully as you can. Don't be embarrassed about your eagerness to understand others' motivations. Ask questions and listen carefully.

We all deserve undivided attention.

Questions

1. Do you try and spend "quality time" with your family? What does this imply about the rest of the time you spend with them?

2. Do you think that "quality time" involves spending money on expensive gifts or experiences? Are these things more meaningful than giving your full attention now?

3. Do you find yourself attending or calling meetings that in the end seem mostly futile?

4. When was the last time you felt completely "on the same page" with someone else? What were you doing? Who were you with?

5. Do you feel that if someone has a view that is opposed to your own, it is your duty to strong-arm them into changing their position?

6. Do you spend as much time listening as you do talking?

7. Do you think leaders should not spend as much time
   listening for fear that they will be considered unsure
   of themselves?

8. Do you think asking questions or listening are signs
   of weakness or strength?

Chapter 10

∞

STAYING IN THE NOW

"Time present and time past
Are both perhaps present in time future,
And time future contained in time past."

—*T.S. Eliot*

If you've read this far, you're perhaps as interested in these ideas as I was when I first discovered the importance of living in the present.

At this point it is possible to focus entirely on the model of the Mission-Driven Mind (page 7) and how we can relate to time in practice. It is the only way I've found to fully grasp how to become time's master rather than resigning ourselves to being its slave.

The Mission-Driven Mind is a healthier and more appropriate way of relating to the world that stems from our understanding of time. We are focused on one priority, and it comes with a sense of inspiration from which we derive a certainty that we're doing the right thing. We are not consumed by incidents in our past, or dreaming of some theoretical future. As we have highlighted in the last three chapters, we take the right action, at the right time, with the right people, for the right reasons.

The central theme running through all the previous chapters is that all the time we will ever have is now. Einstein said, "the distinction between past, present and future is an only an illusion, however persistent." Time only appears to unfold in a linear, uniform sequence. In reality, the future is just a possibility, and the past exists only in our memory. Our perception of time is actually experienced as a series of fleeting instants, a perpetual wave on which we ride the cusp. Our Invisible Clock registers time as the cutting edge of consciousness, already gone by the time we grasp its content. The first question we must ask, therefore, is what exactly must we do to stay in that reality?

Spiritual gurus might say that we need to do nothing at all, just be here in the present, now. Enlightenment will appear as soon as we learn how not to desire it. That might be good for life in a monastery, but less easy to apply in everyday existence.

Motivational speakers, on the other hand, present us with methods built on the sands of enthusiasm. They assure us that we can overcome our psychological barriers usually by replacing our beliefs and emotions—overwhelming as they may be—through a re-feeling or reprogramming process. But in the long term that just adds more conflicting perceptions and thoughts to our memories. These approaches incorrectly presume two things: That we will just conveniently forget that we buried our reality or tried to replace it, and that the psychological past has a logical place in our present.

So, let me restate as simply as I can what I have tried to communicate in previous chapters to be the most practical solution to finding time. We must observe our thoughts with a balanced approach. They are not going away. We should not ignore them, nor should we engage them to the point of distraction.

To summarize:

Become more aware of your own perceptions; observe them closely, and resist the temptation to jump in and label them. It is always possible to become more aware of your perceptions if you quit being the judge and jury. ⧗

Cultivate and possess the focus to do only one thing at a time. Avoid becoming trapped under an avalanche of impressions, more and more abstracted from what is right before your eyes. Fearlessly try to give your full attention to whatever concerns you now.

Finally, tirelessly separate the technical from the psychological, and then ruthlessly ignore the psychological. Except for the technical data needed to solve the immediate circumstance, the past is not relevant now. It is a jumble that will only serve to cloud your vision. Remember, the essential nature of precise timing is to focus on technical information now. I find it useful to tell myself this: See it now, and do only this. Otherwise the moment, and therefore the opportunity, is lost.

Refer again to the illustration of the Mission-Driven Mind (page 7). Do you notice the infinity sign that replaces clock time in the Time-Driven Mind (page 6)? That infinity sign represents the right now we are destined to live in and the creativity that goes along with it when we focus on one priority, feeling inspired. That infinity sign, for all intents and purposes, represents us. And it is infinite; that is, there are no limitations. Instead of trying to define our identity by thinking about our ego, we can instead live who we really are in each instant. There is no need to abstract it or attempt a definition. Each instant the action that we take is us. There is no you or me without us, now.

When we don't alert ourselves beforehand to what thoughts or category of thought we anticipate, the process is straightforward and it allows the right ideas to fall into place. Present vision only happens when our mind is focused without preconceived notions. So, unload your attitudes and opinions and let the thoughts flow. Don't worry, no one else is watching. It takes practice and courage—nobody said it would be easy—but it really is the only way. Practice may be a gentler word than training, but both are euphemisms for discipline, and that is just what is required.

The previous strategies enhance our ability to stay where we want to be, in the now. Let's honestly ask ourselves whether we have become so undisciplined that we enjoy the intrusion of random, unexamined perceptions running through our minds, having become, in effect, gluttons of distraction. The problem is that we mistake thinking about action for action itself.

But how do we really know we are living in the present, or that we are taking action and not just making decisions that we may never put into action? How can we see the difference? The next chapter illuminates the five spheres that define the integrative action of a Mission-Driven Mind.

Chapter 11

∞

THE FIVE SPHERES OF ACTION

"Life well spent is long."

—*Leonardo daVinci*

In this last chapter, we will see how we can put everything we have learned into practical, everyday use. We have already developed the ability to focus ourselves in the present, which is the essential, all-important step. From there we can get results by framing and acting on what we want to do now. After all, living in the moment isn't living for the moment. We must take action and it must be integrative, and inclusive.

The symbol of action is the five spheres, a tool we can use to gain a better understanding of what we think we should do. It essentially helps us answer two questions. The first is whether or not what we have in mind is really an action, or a thought about another thought that makes us feel good about what we think, like the diet we will begin tomorrow. The second is whether or not the action in question is the right action for us. The last thing we want to do is fool ourselves and run headlong down the wrong path.

If we look honestly at each of the five spheres, we will see the right action. All we will need to do is take it.

The following are the five component spheres that we need to consider to be certain of our actions. Each contributes a vital set of questions and parameters that are essential to clearly seeing the whole picture.

ASSESSMENT

This sphere looks at the people factors. What's the status of both my personal situation and that of the other personnel? Where do we stand? In other words, what about me and the people involved with me?

Fig. 4: The five spheres of integrative action

DEFINITION

What are my detailed, specific objectives? If I can't nail them down, then I know I can't be serious.

PURPOSE

What are my stated goals? What do I want to accomplish with my action? This deals not only with the actions themselves but how they fit in to the overall scheme of what I'm doing.

IMPACT

What do I intend to have happen? In response to our every action we can be reasonably sure there is going to be a reaction that affects us and those around us. What is it likely to be? Is that really my intention?

MISSION

Is what I'm about to do part of my mission in life? The consideration about mission concerns a deeper relationship with life and the world around us. What purpose do I serve? Who am I and why am I doing this? How does my mission fit in with the group mission that I'm on? ⧗

There are two broad components to the mission sphere. The first is about our standards of individual and corporate virtue. The second concerns a larger, in fact, the ultimate question. What is my mission in life? If I'm not on a mission, then why not? Aren't we all important enough to be on a mission? Not a role, a job, or even a career, but a real mission. We must ask ourselves if we don't know already. Why not me? If we have no answer to this question, we must begin to seriously contemplate it (always keeping in mind the distinction between a mission and considerations of the ego). Because without this step, there will be no successful fulfillment of the five spheres.

Since the five spheres are designed for very practical use, the best way to proceed is by looking at three case studies.

EXHIBIT 1.

Suppose we are at war, and, as Supreme

Commander, we need to make a decision about

whether or not to attack and secure Hill X.

Let us examine each aspect of the decision

by applying the five spheres.

Sphere 1, assessment. Personal and personnel.

Who is involved? How prepared am I? What is

the status of my soldiers' morale? What about

the opposing forces?

Sphere 2, definition. Our objective. What do we want to

do? Define it. In this case, we want to have

effective control of the hill, which translates into

2000 soldiers with 750,000 rounds of ammuni-

tion in place for 72 hours.

Sphere 3, purpose. Our goals. What is the purpose? We want to have the strategic advantage over a valley that controls access to a pass through a mountain range.

Sphere 4, impact. The organization and the organism (me). How will this impact the army and my ability to command? The army will then be able to further coordinate the attack on the war zone by moving additional reinforcements to the front. Then I will have extended my strategic options as commander.

Sphere 5, mission. Restate the mission. What is it? The mission is to win the war. That depends upon our ability to engage and defeat the enemy in battles that will be fought, contingent upon this essential victory.

Conclusion. The circle of action is now complete. The time to strike is now.

EXHIBIT 2.

Now let's look at a corporate case study: ABC Co. has begun an English Language training program. We have been informed that management is very pleased with the results since all reports from the participants have been positive.

Sphere 1, assessment. Both the teachers and students have reported consistently that the program is very successful and rewarding. Good marks for this sphere.

Sphere 2, definition. The classes are for the most part conversational and therefore do not have any specific objectives that can be defined or tested. No one knows exactly which students are at what level. Mediocre marks for this sphere.

Sphere 3, purpose. This is a voluntary program, so although about the same number of students attend each session, those in charge are not sure if the same persons attend each session. It is therefore not possible to talk about a defined percentage of the workforce learning the target language as a program goal. Bad marks for this sphere.

Sphere 4, impact. Since the organization is a local manufacturer and distributor of a single consumer product, the value added to the organization internally is questionable. In fact, it may be achieving high marks on level one because the employees are gaining a skill that will enable them to leave the company for higher paying jobs. Not very smart.

Sphere 5, mission. The overall mission of the company to sell product locally is apparently not being affected by the language-training program.

Conclusion. Why is this program still being funded? At the very least, it needs to be revised if it is to continue.

EXHIBIT 3.

Let us take a look at an example on the individual level. Mr. Y sees an MBA as a possible goal. He is very excited about this idea initially, but let's take a look at what happens when he takes his idea and tests it with the spheres.

Sphere 1, assessment. I am very excited about going back to school for my MBA. I want to learn more. My wife is concerned about my making that commitment, and my kids think it's funny that I'm going back to school.

Sphere 2, definition. My objective is to get an MBA in two years of night school at a local university.

Sphere 3, purpose. My goals are the following: I want a new job, more money, and more respect. I want to reinvent myself.

Sphere 4, impact. Well, if I get an MBA, I will have the opportunity to take on more responsibility and make more money, a temptation for me personally, but it will sacrifice family activities. My wife and kids think I'm educated enough and would rather see more of me than have more stuff.

Sphere 5, mission. I never really asked myself this
question before. But now that I have, to be honest, I'm actually pretty happy and my family is
my priority. I've changed my mind about the
MBA, at least for now.

Conclusion. This example illustrates what happens
when someone clearly sees what he wants to
do. The action becomes apparent when he runs
through each of the five spheres. He finally
takes a good look at what is important in his life.

In the third case study, Mr. Y had never really considered
his mission in life before now. Many people have trouble
with the idea of a personal mission, assuming that it is a
goal only for exceptional achievers. But that is simply
untrue. Everyone is here for a reason, and none of those
reasons are less important than others. What are your pas-
sions? Is it to be a great mom? To own your own busi-
ness? To inspire others in a classroom? What really gets
your blood pumping? What satisfies you the most?

There are no right or wrong answers. And, for most
of us, the answers will not all come right away. But if we
stay focused on the present, it is possible to find strength

and certainty in each instant. Remember, now is all we have. Stay in each moment, and bring full attention to every action taken.

Because, in the final analysis, your mission is not what you write down, but what you bring to each instant and give of yourself. Only you can bring the unique qualities in you to bear on each moment.

Not one sphere can be missing in defining the right action and completing the mission. And when the five spheres are integrated into a continuous circle, they form a star in the center.

The ultimate lesson in understanding time is that you exist in it for a reason. In the end, you are the mission. And when you take the right action, you are that star.

Put down this book and harness your potential in each passing instant. Now is your time to shine.

Bibliography

Barbour, Julian. *The End of Time; The Next Revolution in Physics.* Oxford: Oxford University Press, 1999.

Barrow, John. *Theories of Everything.* Oxford: Oxford University Press, 1992.

Berlinski, David. *Newton's Gift: How Sir Isaac Newton Unlocked the System of the World.* New York: Free Press, 2000.

Brand, Chris. *The G Factor: General Intelligence and Its Implications.* New York: John Wiley, 1996.

Coveney, Peter and Highfield, Roger. *The Arrow of Time.* London: Flamingo, 1991.

Dancy, Jonathan. *Perceptual Knowledge.* Oxford: Oxford University Press, 1988.

Davies, Paul. *About Time: Einstein's Unfinished Revolution.* London: Penguin Press, 1995.

Egan, Kieran. *The Educated Mind, How Cognitive Tools Shape Our Understanding.* Chicago: Chicago University Press, 1997.

Eddington, Authur. *Time and Gravitation.* Cambridge: Cambridge University Press, 1920.

Einstein, Albert. *Relativity: The Special and the General Theory. A Popular Exposition.* London: Routledge, 1960.

Frazer, Gordon. *The Search for Infinity: Solving the Mysteries of the Universe.* New York: Facts on File, 1995.

Friedman, William J. *About Time: Inventing the Fourth Dimension.* Cambridge: MIT Press, 1990.

Gardet, Louis. *Cultures and Time.* Paris: Unesco Press, 1976.

Goleman, Daniel. *Emotional Intelligence.* New York: Bantam Books, 1995.

Griffiths, Paul E. *What Emotions Really Are: The Problem Of Psychological Categories.* Chicago: University Of Chicago Press, 1997.

Hunt, Harry T. *On the Nature of Consciousness: Cognitive, Phenomenological, and Transpersonal Perspectives.* New Haven: Yale University Press, 1995.

BIBLIOGRAPHY

Krishnamurti, J. *The Awakening of Intelligence*. London: V. Gollancz, 1973.

_____. *The Ending of Time*. London: V. Gollancz, 1988.

_____. Bohm, David., ed. *The Only Revolution*. London: V. Gollancz, 1970.

Lewontin, Richard C. *The Triple Helix; Gene, Organism, and Environment*. Cambridge: Harvard University Press, 2000.

Ornstein, Robert E. *On the Experience of Time*. Boulder: West View Press, 1997.

Perkins, David N. *Outsmarting IQ: The Emerging Science of Learnable Intelligence*. New York: Free Press, 1995.

Pinker, Steven. *How The Mind Works*. New York: W.W. Norton, 1997.

Stachel, Jon J., ed. *The Collected Papers of Albert Einstein*. Princeton: Princeton University Press, 1987.

Strachey, James., ed. *Sigmund Freud: The Ego and Id*. London: Hogarth Press, 1962.

Zee, A. *Fearful Symmetry: The Search for Beauty in Modern Physics*. New York: Macmillan Publishing Company, 1986.

Index